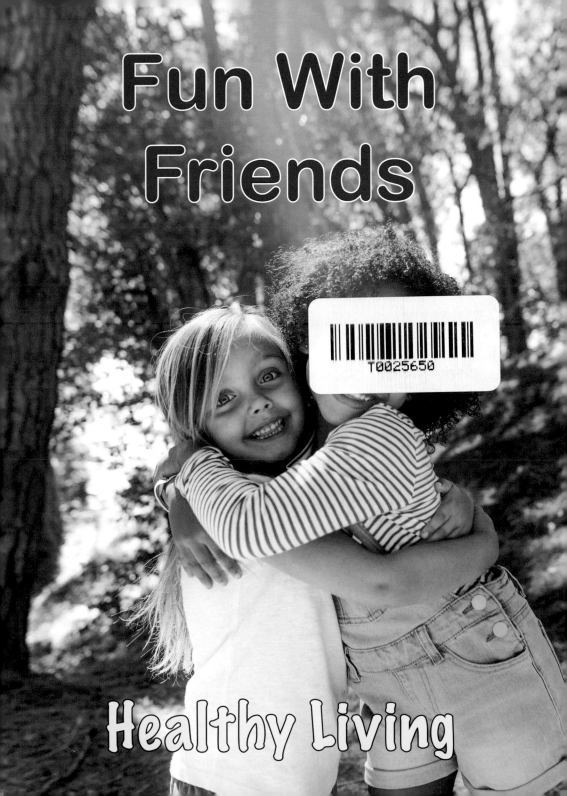

Fun With Friends

T0025650

Healthy Living

Here are my friends.

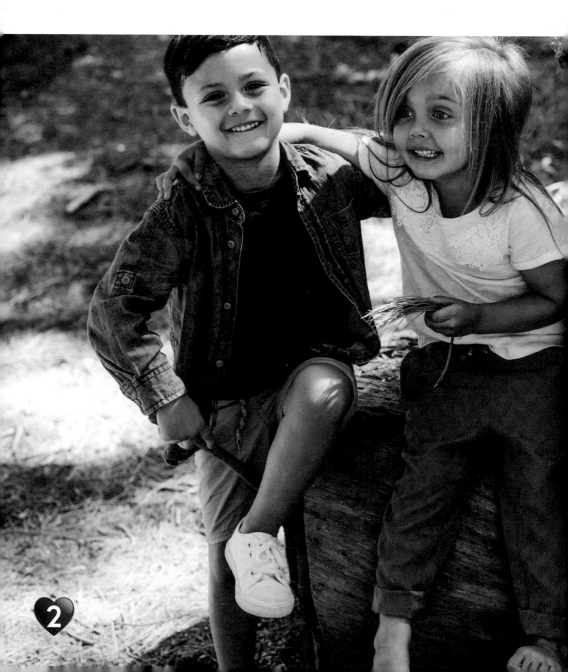

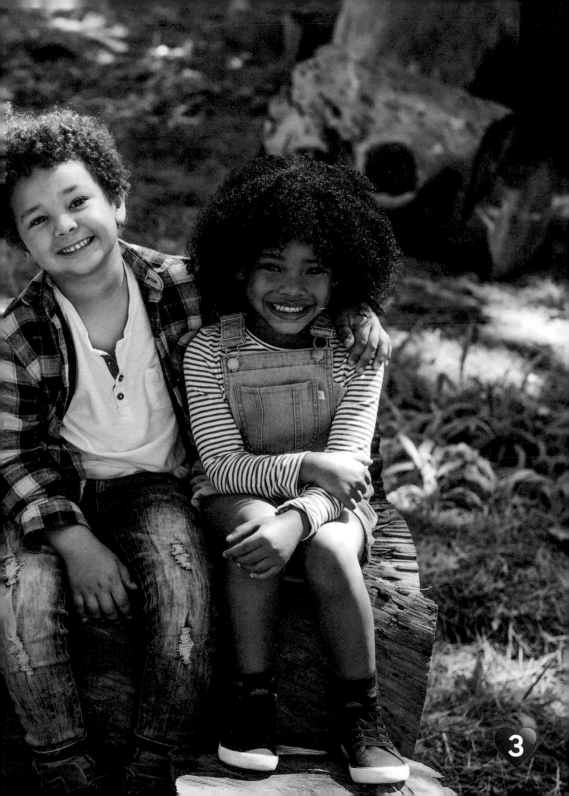

We have fun together.

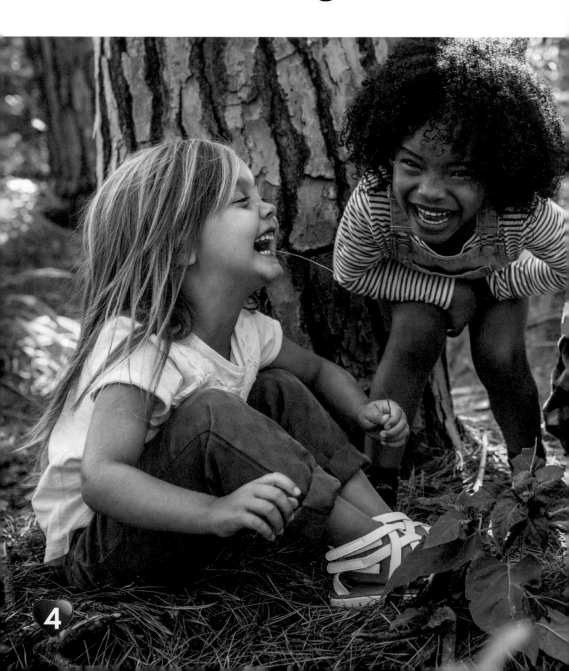

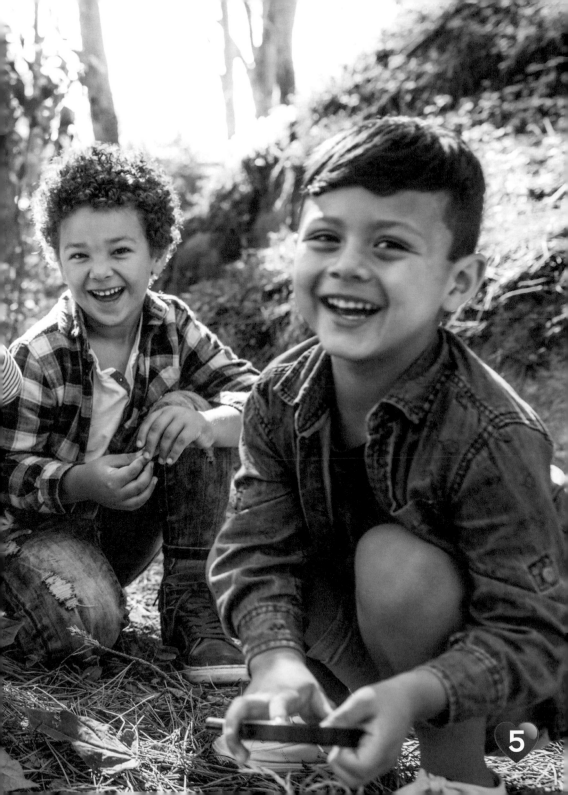

5

We play together.

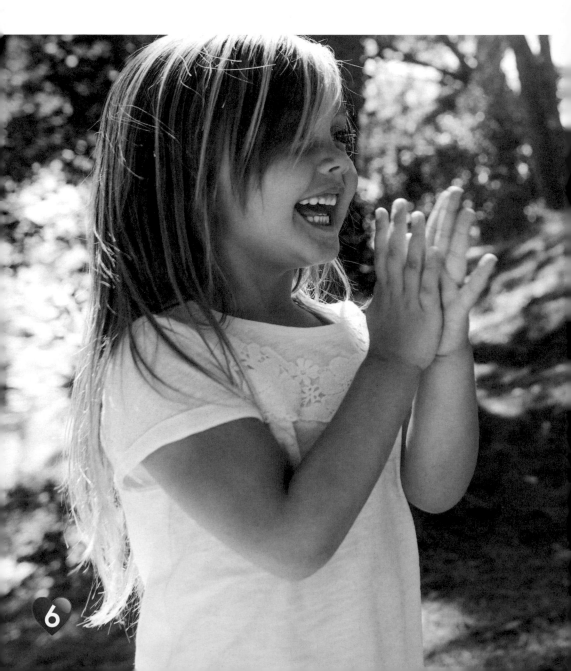

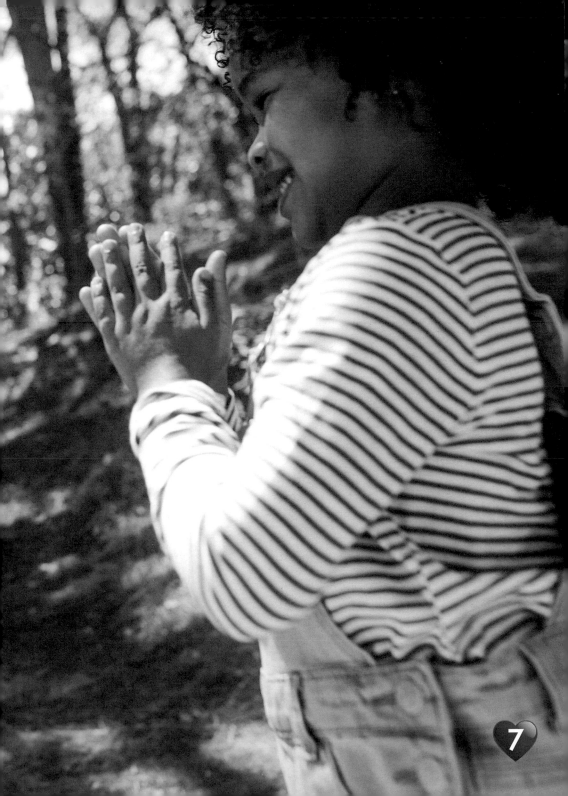

We work together.

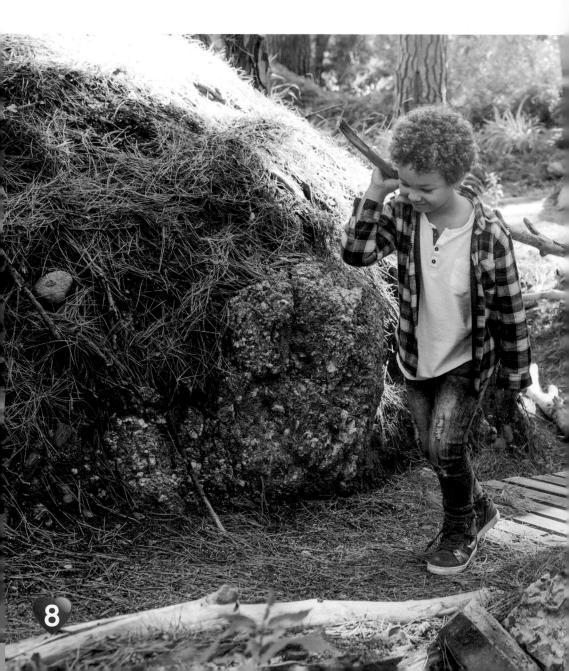

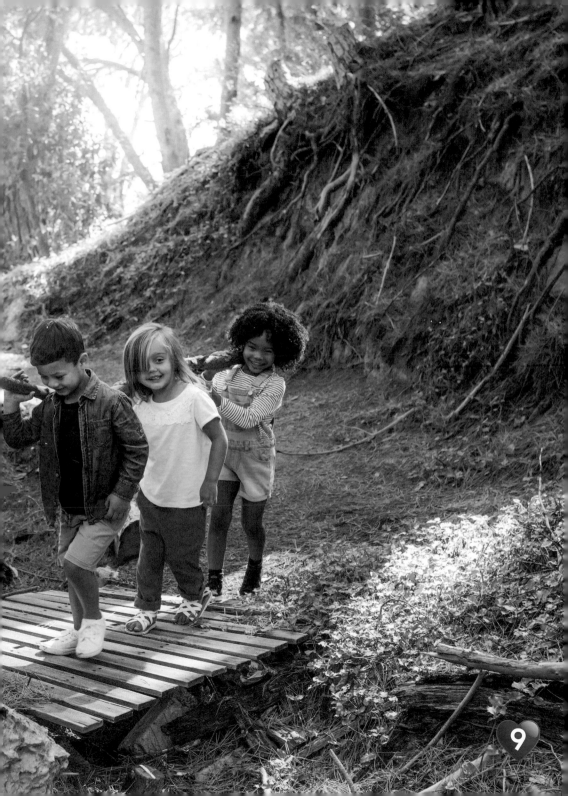

We play games.

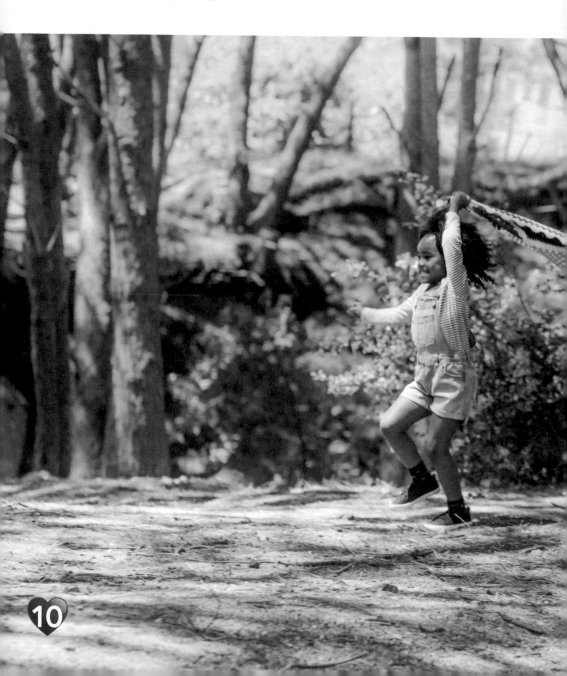

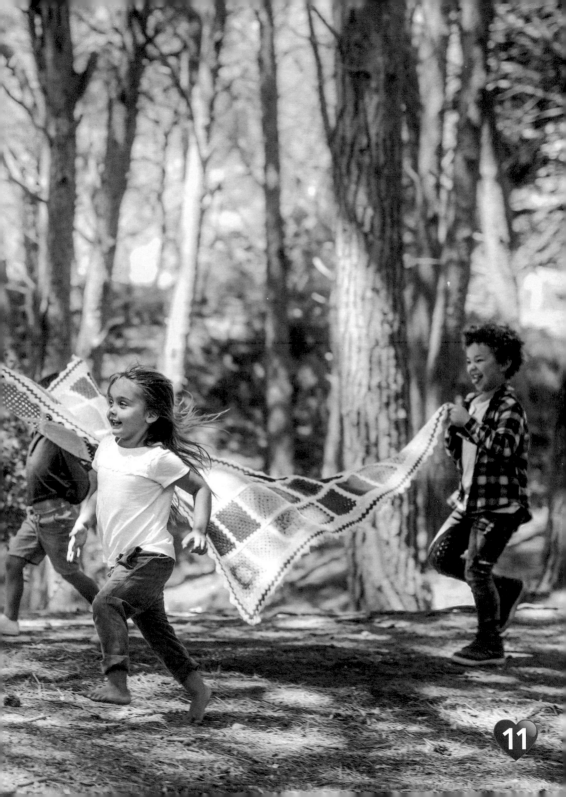

We play hide and seek.

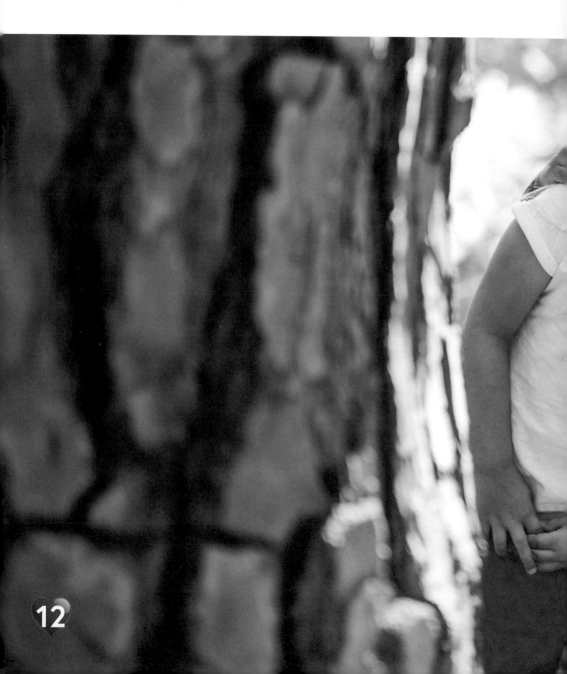

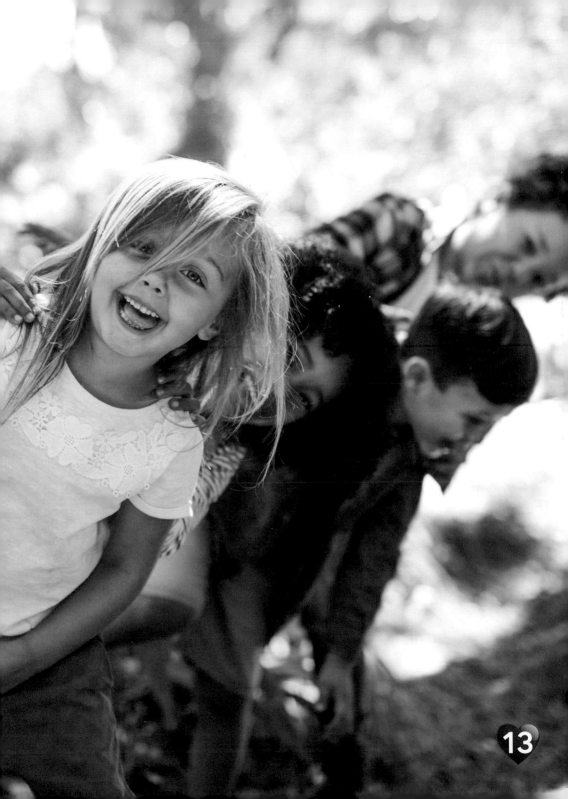

Look at the bubbles!

We blow bubbles together.

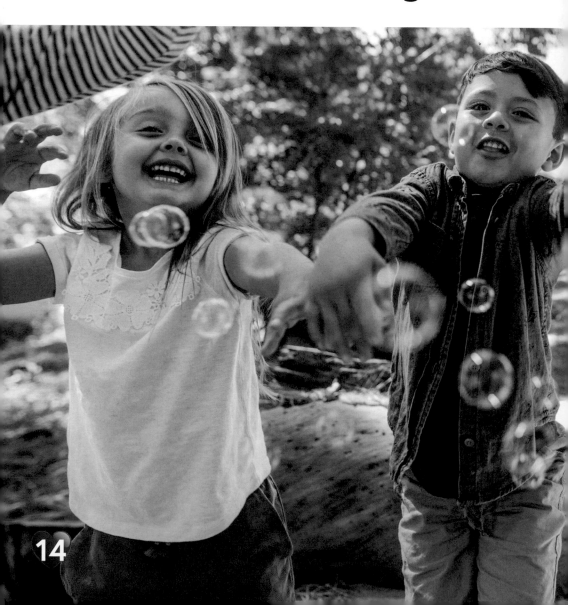

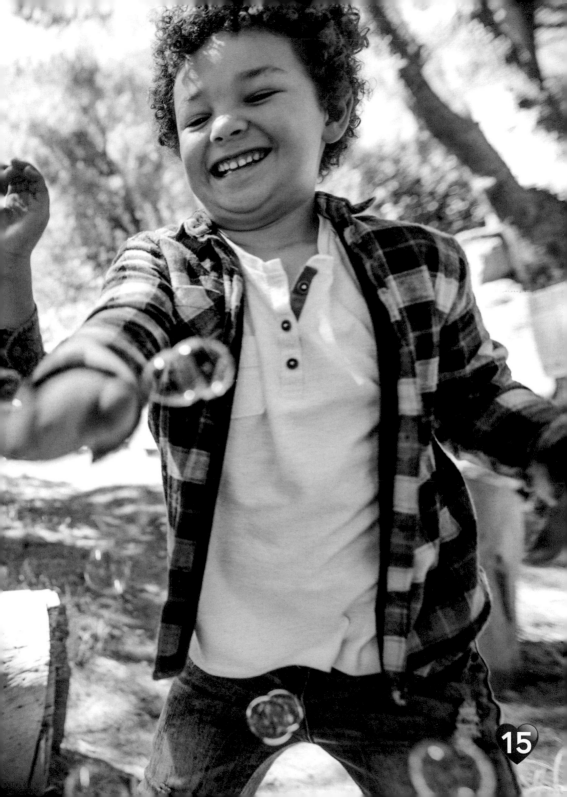

We have fun

when we are together.

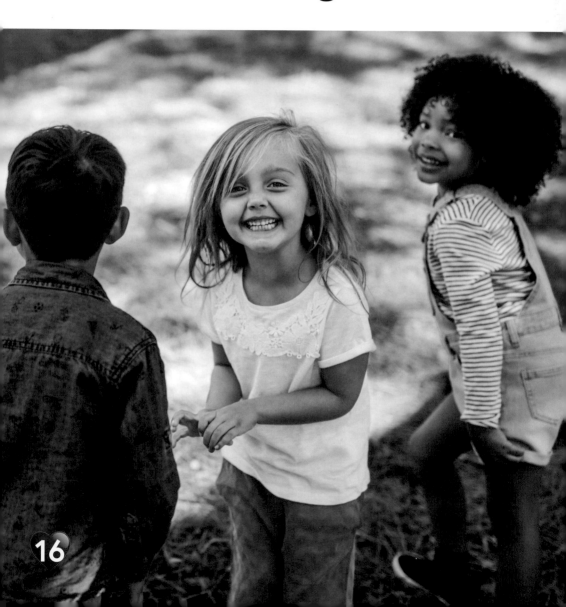